The United Kingdom Literacy Association

formerly The United Kingdom Reading Association

Literature Circles:
Better Talking, More Ideas

By Carole King and Jane Briggs

Minibook 19

UKRA Minibook Series

Series Editor Susan Ellis

Past series editors Alison B. Littlefair, Bobbie Neate, Ros Fisher

Published minibooks

Genres in the Classroom Alison B. Littlefair

Running Family Reading Groups Sue Beverton, Ann Stuart, Morag Hunter-Carsch and Cecelia Oberist

Miscue Analysis in the Classroom Robin Campbell

Teaching Handwriting Peter Smith

Teaching Spelling Brigid Smith

Supporting Struggling Readers Diana Bentley and Dee Reid

Phonological Awareness Frances James

Exploring the Writing of Genres Beverley Derewianka

The Power of Words Norma Mudd

Reading to Find Out Helen Arnold

Moving Towards Literacy with Environmental Print Linda Miller

Guided Reading Jo Makgill

English as an Additional Language Constant Leung

Developing Writing 7 - 13 Roy Corden

Poetry Matters Andrew Lambirth

Children's Writing Journals Lynda Graham and Annette Johnson

Tell Me Another... Speaking, Listening and Learning Through Storytelling Jacqueline Harrett

Drama: Reading, Writing and Speaking Our Way Forward Teresa Grainger and Angela Pickard

Issue number 19:
Literature Circles:
Better Talking, More Ideas
Issue Authors: Carole King and Jane Briggs
Series Editor: Susan Ellis

Published 2005
ISBN 1 897638 33 7
ISSN 1350-7664

Published by U‹LA
United Kingdom Literacy Association.
Upton House, 4 Baldock Street, Royston,
Hertfordshire, SG8 5AY England

The United Kingdom Reading Association (UKRA) became the United Kingdom Literacy Association (UKLA) on May 25th 2003.

Literature Circles: Better Talking, More Ideas

Contents

Introduction   1

1. Where it all began   2

2. Setting up literature circles   10

3. Literature circles
    with younger children   22

4. Literature circles
    with 8-11 year olds   30

    Bibliography   40

I think that the creature is a dog and she is pregnant.
I think that the people who keep knocking on the door will make some-
think bad happen.
I think all the dogs friends and family will be caught and
killed and ~~the~~ the dog will be left all alone.
I think the soldiers will catch the dog and lock her up. Fleabane
will get hungry and come out of the den and will wander
off into the wild and won't be able to find the den again.
He will find a pack of wolves and ~~you~~ stay with them
then ~~the dog Fleabane~~ will escape and try to find Fleabane.
                                                    and abused
The dog finds Fleabane but gots chased away by the
wolves.
I think Fleabane will go hunting at night with out
his mother's permission and walk into the wildcat's
teritory and comes back to his mother injured.

Learning to lift the words off the page

We learn to do something by doing it and reading is no exception. If, through literature circles children engage with reading, they are likely to read more. This will certainly improve their ability to use all three cueing systems (semantic, syntactic and graphophonic) as well as increase their sight vocabulary. Reading aloud with expression can help children in their search for meaning. Often children's ability to read aloud with expression improves as they begin to enjoy entertaining other members of their literature circle group through their reading.

Developing strategies and competencies through exploratory talk

Group discussion and interaction is an important learning strategy for all children. Older children often need to focus on the process of using talk to learn. For example, in the National Curriculum for England and Wales at Key Stage 2 (pupils aged 8-11 years), explicit reference is made to the need for pupils to be taught to *'vary contributions to suit the activity and purpose, including exploratory and tentative comments where ideas are being collected together, and reasoned, evaluative comments as discussion moves to conclusions a or actions'* (DfEE/QCA, 1999, p. 22).

The example of children's talk at the start of this chapter demonstrates the kind of intimate and tentative conversations between children, which capture *'The ebb and flow of spoken thoughts and feelings'* (Britton et al 1975, p.10). Britton describes such talk as language in the expressive mode and stresses its importance:

'Its function in one sense is to be with. To be with people. To explore the relationships. To extend the togetherness of situations. It's the language of ordinary face-to-face speech. So it's our means of coming together with other people out of our essential separateness. But it's also the language in which we first-draft most of our important ideas' (Britton, 1982, p. 97).

This exploratory talk depends upon opportunities to use language in the [expressi]ve mode, for as Barnes says, exploratory talk is *'often hesitant [and inc]omplete; it enables the speaker to try out new ideas, to hear how [they sou]nd, to see what others make of them, to arrange information and ideas into different patterns'* (1976, p. 126).

Discussion within literature circles can help children to read for meaning. As one child remarked, *'When you're on your own you can't speak. You [have to re]ly on yourself for what's happening.'* The opportunity to voice [ideas in a] context where all personal contributions are valued, enables [readers to] negotiate a joint construction of the meaning of the story on many levels. Reader response theory stresses the dialogic nature of the reading process and expressive talk facilitates the transaction needed between the meanings readers bring to, and take from, the text (Rosenblatt, 1978). Unless readers are able to bring their own experiences to their reading to predict, hypothesise, picture, compare, assess and evaluate, they are unlikely to fully engage with the texts they read. Through reading and discussing a text, children articulate these processes, recognise what they do as readers and why, and learn from what others say.

The following extract, taken from Paul (1995), illustrates these points. The discussion occurred as a class of five and six year olds were working in literature circle groups. Notice how, in the absence of teacher interrogation, the way that the children find their own voices. The group are reading Trouble with the Tucker Twins (Impey, 1992). The children chose this story "because there were twins in the class". Early in the story, the twins are bullying a boy and the literature circle group are discussing this:

Lily   *Why doesn't he tell the teacher? I did when some one was being horrible to me in the playground and the teacher stopped them and they didn't do it again*

John   *Maybe he did and they haven't put it in the book*

Rosie   *Maybe he's just sticking up for himself for a minute*

Grace   *The Tucker twins are being nasty to him. They're cutting up his paper and making so much noise that he doesn't want to go to school*

Lily	*I said that at the beginning*
Rosie	*They are whispering to each other cos they're going to do something horrible to him*

Lily's initial question is the result of bringing her own experiences to the story. In answering it, John and Rosie offer different hypotheses. John recognises, albeit implicitly, the choices authors have when writing and shows also the way that young children enter the world of the text in such a way that the main character takes on a life of his own outside of the story. Grace uses the picture to give additional detail, which gives Lily the satisfaction of confirming the importance of her earlier observation and question. Finally, Rosie predicts what will happen next. Later, all is resolved when the bullied boy realises that the twins are only bullies when they are together. He makes friends with first one and then both of the twins. Rosie shows the importance both of being able to identify with the characters and of knowing what she likes to read and why. She says:

The story was sad at the beginning but then it ended up happier at the end. I wish it was happy right through because I don't like sad books, cos they make me sad but I keep reading it to make sure they are going to be happy.

This short analysis of the varied responses made by the children indicates that reading is indeed a complex process. Readers need both to create the world of the text from the symbols and pictures on the pages and follow the narrative threads, but, as Rosie implies, we read stories for emotional reasons, to find out what happens, hoping that all problems will be resolved to our satisfaction. The pressure on teachers teaching young children to read often means that this important aspect of the reading process is lost. For example, curriculum guidance in guided reading at Key Stage One of the National Curriculum for England and Wales is principally designed to enable teachers to intervene to help children read the words more effectively (DfEE 1998). As demonstrated above, the small group situation also provides an ideal opportunity for children to use exploratory talk to develop as active and collaborative readers who seek meaning that is satisfying both cognitively and affectively. As one eight year old reader explained, '*I like group reading because we can share ideas together.... It is like working in a team.*'

Reading, Thinking and Talking

Meek suggests that real reading *'is a kind of inner speech and is bound to have a marked effect on the growth of the mind of the reader'* (1982, p. vii). This point is illustrated by Christine, who, after reading *The Tunnel* (Browne, 1997), explained 'in my head I thought that the girl would have to use a spell to save him'. When children in a literature circle share their stories and find out what others have to say about the same stories, they develop their awareness of the inner speech that all readers develop and, through this, learn how to be a more effective reader. The 'inner speech' of children often surprises teachers. A newly qualified teacher, trying the literature circle approach for the first time was surprised at the complexity of the children's thoughts:

'I was taken aback by how much there was to say from the cover before we had even begun to read the book and it made me realise that these thoughts and feelings would usually never be verbalised'
(Graham, 1999).

Another teacher on the same project was amazed at how difficult some children found it to picture the story in their heads. In the past she had assumed that this was something automatic, and had believed that *'everyone did'* (ibid.).

Being part of a literature circle can change how children read. After six months of participating in a literature circle group, Amy commented, *'I don't just read the book, I think about it now'* (King and Robinson, 1993). This is a significant change. It demonstrates that Amy had internalised the talk process that had happened during her circle time and had become a more thoughtful reader. Amy was not alone in this. It was an observation made by many other children involved. For them, the literature circle had enabled them to work in what the Russian psychologist Vygotsky called a zone of proximal development (1978, p. 86). Working with a text that engaged and challenged them as readers, and with the guidance of the teacher in the form of active participation or journal response and encouragement, the children were able to explore both the texts and the reading process in ways they would not have been able to manage independently. As Vygotsky suggests: 'Every function of the child's cultural development appears on two levels: first on the social and later the psychological level. First, between people as an interpersonal category and then inside the child as an intra-personal category' (ibid, p. 57). In the literature circle, the interpersonal dialogic nature of the talk was then internalised to become part of the independent thinking applied to texts read alone or with younger siblings.

The following unsolicited and entirely unexpected conversation with 10 year-olds evolved from a discussion about what makes it easy to get into a book. It demonstrates that, when children are really given the chance to talk about what and how they read, they discover for themselves what they need to do.

Brad   *There's a saying, "It's not eyes with books, its head and eyes with books" Like it's head goes to eyes, cos some people just read with their eyes but you have to read with head and eyes*

Teacher *Where did you learn that?*

Brad   *Well I just thought of it*

Teacher *It has to be the head and eyes. What does he mean Kate?*

Kate   *You have to think about it with your head and not just read it with your eyes*

Teacher *Do you mean some people might just read the words off without any thought?*

Brad   *Yeah. That's what I mean*

Teacher *Do you ever remember reading like that, with eyes only?*

Brad   *Yes*

Mike   *In the infants*

Teacher *How do you know you did it like that?*

Mike   *Well I didn't think about the books much then I just read them*

Teacher *Just the words?*

Mike   *Yes*

Chapter 2

Setting Up Literature Circles

Literature circles work best when the teacher has thought carefully about what she wants to achieve, how she will introduce the idea of a literature circle, and the type of texts to use.

The texts used for literature circles are important. Books from reading schemes simply do not offer the rich opportunities for active, creative reading that are offered by quality picture books and novels. We found that the texts need to be selected to:

- interesting to children
- extend children as readers by introducing them to new authors and different genres
- be multi-layered (polysemic) so that they can be discussed at different levels and from different perspectives
- provide variety, including picture books for older readers and books that reflect children's popular culture (Meek, 1988).

The teacher needs to:
- know the experiences and attitudes that children need to possess to become readers, as well as the strategies and competencies
- understand the centrality of the role of expressive exploratory talk for learning
- understand the role of the text in learning to read and how texts are constructed at all levels
- model for the whole class, what it means to be a member of a literature circle. This includes ways of talking and writing about what the children read and how to operate independently as a group (Robinson and King, 1995)

- organise additional support for children: It helps to have parents' support and perhaps Teaching Assistants or Learning Support Supervisors to help those who are more reluctant or less able readers to keep up with their peer group
- be both observer and participant member of the circle at least for the first and last session, without being overly directive
- think about how to encourage children to respond to each other in group talk, without always waiting for the teacher to intervene
- encourage shy children to respond by providing for paired talk first to give confidence
- introduce, encourage and support the use of reading journals (where this is appropriate for the age-group).

All children who participate in a literature circle need to know that everyone is taking the idea seriously. This means that older children need to commit themselves to:
- completing the agreed reading before the next session
- keeping a journal to continue the dialogue whilst not a member of the circle (if appropriate)
- being a supportive and co-operative group member.

Each literature circle group needs to meet for least one period each week. The children read most of the text during silent reading time in class, or at home. They should use the group time for talking about their thoughts, reactions and the issues raised in their journals. Thus, children set the agenda and the teacher's input nudges them to attend to specific aspects, such as narrative viewpoint.

There needs to be some expectation that everyone in the literature circle group will be able to read and engage with the chosen text. Less able children can often read the text with support and gain enormously from being part of the group and from discussing their reading with others. Younger children must not be allowed to believe that reading aloud is the most important aspect of the literature circle (although literature circles do improve this aspect).

Getting started

This is the process that we used to get started, working within the context of the National Curriculum for England and Wales. It shows one way to start a literature circle approach. Although it may look a little didactic at first, we found that it often helps to have a strong framework at the beginning. As both the teacher and the children get used to working in this way, the framework can be modified to make some aspects more open-ended and to ensure that the literature circle is meeting the needs of the children, the texts and the teacher.

Younger children may go through the same steps as older children to work in their literature circle, but will often finish the book in one session. It is often helpful to let younger children begin by telling the story from the pictures alone and then reading the text, or having the text read to them, to see if they were right. Don't be afraid to return to the text in the next session for further reading and discussion, even if the children read through to the end in the first session.

Lesson One:

Begin by asking your group what kinds of books they like to read, their favourite titles and authors and their reasons for liking or disliking a book. This should be a brief discussion to enable you to learn something about their preferences.

Ask the children what makes a good reader, and what they think good readers do and think about as they read. Note down the answers and come back to them at the end of the session.

Hand out the books you have selected, but do not allow the children to open them. Spend time discussing the title, the cover, the contents pages or the chapter titles. This helps the children to think about the likely story content, reminds them of any relevant experiences and encourages them to begin to predict what the story might be about. It will help them to be active and creative in making sense of the text if they can easily draw on their own experiences and their memories of other stories they know. You may want to jot down some of the children's expectations for future reference, and as a way of modelling journal writing.

Read the first few paragraphs of the story aloud, stopping to discuss the illustrations if appropriate. It is often hard for children to begin reading a new text with expression when they have little idea of what the story is about. If the teacher reads the first part aloud, it enables the children to get the 'tune of the language' used so that the story makes better sense. Margaret Meek (1991) argues that competent readers tolerate uncertainty when they begin a new text, genre or author whereas less competent readers need help to do this. Often, by reading the first few paragraphs aloud, the teacher is helping such children to cope with this uncertainty rather than give up.

Let the children take it in turns to read. Don't insist that they all read aloud if it is clear that some group members feel threatened. You could suggest that you read the text with a reluctant reader, or ask children to read aloud in pairs. You will probably find that the other group members are very supportive.

When everyone has read, stop and ask the children to jot down what is in their head at that moment about the book (or, if you are not using reading journals, talk about it). Then ask them to share their thoughts with their neighbour before explaining their comments to the whole group. Look for opportunities to help the children articulate what they do when they read. Explain to the children that you want them to talk to, support and respond to, each other. One way of doing this is to model the type of interactions by  saying, "Mark. What do you think of what Jane has just said?" You may find initially that Mark is surprised to be asked but if you do this several times, the children will realise that their role is to listen and respond to each other, not just the adult. Praise those who do.

Responding as Readers

When children talk or write about the story, and voice their thoughts about reading, they have different types of responses, each of which is valuable. The examples below illustrate some of these responses, drawn from children's entries in their reading journals and from transcripts of discussion during the literature circle.

Children need to bring their own experiences to the text to make sense of it:
Nicky had to guess what the man's name was and the man had loads of sweets in his compartment. I wonder if the man is going to give Nicky some sweets.
I remember when two girls were murdered in Wild Park and a boy went far away and a man was in his car and he left the boy in a far off place and came back all bony and bare.
(Ashley, 10 years)

Children need to predict what might happen next, and why to help them structure their reading by looking for clues in the text and to make them want to read on:
I think that something interesting and nice is going to happen because they have started on adventures already.
(Lewis, 8 years)

Children need to share their rich mental pictures to help them learn from each other how to do this:
I have a picture of him finding his brother" (demonstrates how he looks)
"I could see fire around Starjik but not- ice. I thought it would be a big ice palace and them throwing them and then thinking "What if this does- n't work?"
(Dwayne, 10 years)

Children need to empathise by saying what they feel about the characters to identify with them:

He shouldn't go with strangers. I hope he don't. I wonder who Nick thinks it is?

(Rebeka, 10 years)

Children need to assess what makes them keep reading to articulate what makes a good story:

I hope they solve the mystery soon or get another clue because they are finding out things all the time and hardly any clues so I would like them to find some more clues.

(Samuel, 8 years)

Children need to evaluate why the text is like it is, and why it works to help them to develop critical reading skills:

I like it when it starts. It doesn't go 'one day' or 'once upon a time'. Like, it goes "It had rained every day since grandma arrived in London". Its good, the way it started.

(Janey, 10 years)

Children need to seek clarification and re-read to realise the significance of particular words:

Jackie   *Where's the picture where it says "not now love maybe…"?*

Nathan *I read that didn't I?*

Jackie   *Did he say "Not now love"?*

Nathan *Yes*

Teacher (checking the actual text on the page) *No. (it just says) "not now".*

Jackie   *No. Because it seemed to say…* (Teacher and J re-read the text) *Happy Birthday love!*

Teacher *Oh Yes. Why do you think that made such a difference? Why did you point that out to me?*

Jackie   *It shows that he's more… happier.*

(Jackie and Nathan, 8 years with their teacher)

Children need to compare events and characters with those in other stories or films to help them to make meaning:
The puff adder is a bit like the snake who tempted Eve to eat the fruit off the tree of knowledge. I think the creature is a dragon.
(Louise, 10 years)

Children need to identify themes and ideas to make wider and deeper sense of their reading:
Hannah's problem is her father. He works too much to care about her. The animals and the girl are both in prison.
(Charlotte, 9 years)

Children need to ask questions to clarify their thinking, become critical readers and help them to become more involved in the text:
Who is the ghost? I think it is great uncle Barnaby. Why don't I know anything about Troy?
(Robert, 10 years)

Helping children to respond in these ways helps them to realise how the words on the page work in their heads. Encouraging children to use evidence from the text as well as evidence from their own experiences to support their ideas helps them to see that reading a story or poem is a bit like being a detective, looking for the clues that the author has left. Close attention to the words used helps them to see how the writer creates the world of the text. One useful question to ask is, 'How does your brain know that's what you think?' (King and Robinson, 1993).

Although the literature circle sessions are not tightly planned in terms of specific learning intentions, the teacher often sees potential to develop the children's responses in particular ways. It is important to remember that the children's agenda should always be encouraged and that their response may open-up areas for development never envisaged by the teacher.

Independent reading

At a certain point in the session, ask the children to read the next paragraph or page by themselves and set a question for them to think about. The question should be open-ended and encourage many diffei answers. Quicker readers can be asked to think of their o' questions. Invite children to respond to what they have read, responses to particular aspects if appropriate. Finally, negotiate how far the group will read before the next literature circle session.

Subsequent sessions

Initially children and their teacher should begin by sharing their responses to their reading since the last session. To do this, they may like to refer to their reading journal, if they have been keeping one. The reading then continues as before.

Reading Journals

At their simplest, reading journals are notebooks where pupils jot down their responses to their reading, as they read. This is the kind of writing which, until fairly recently, has been neglected in school as a way of learning (Graham, 1999). When showing children how to write readin encourage them to be honest and to use expressive language nearest to speech (Britton, 1992).

Initially pupils may simply retell the story in their reading journals. This is a valuable way of making sense of their reading but it is limiting. The teacher, by sharing her own reading journal with the group, and by prompting a range of responses during the discussion, can encourage pupils to respond to their reading in all the ways shown earlier in this chapter.

Hannah wontit to go to the
Zoo But She wovoot
alwaD to go to the Zoo
She went to Bed
and She 1voow the
GORILLA on the flov
and it doe Biga and
Biga then it wentto
the Botoom of the
Bed and the GoRiuLA
and She went swigin.
on the triy

Fig 1: Initially children may simply re-tell the story

The children may also illustrate characters in their reading journals, re-write endings, or add bits they consider to be missing from the original story. Some children like to draw maps, diagrams or family trees to sort out journeys, events and relationships. Others use the reading journal to comment on their own responses to the story, or to say what they enjoyed about the book:

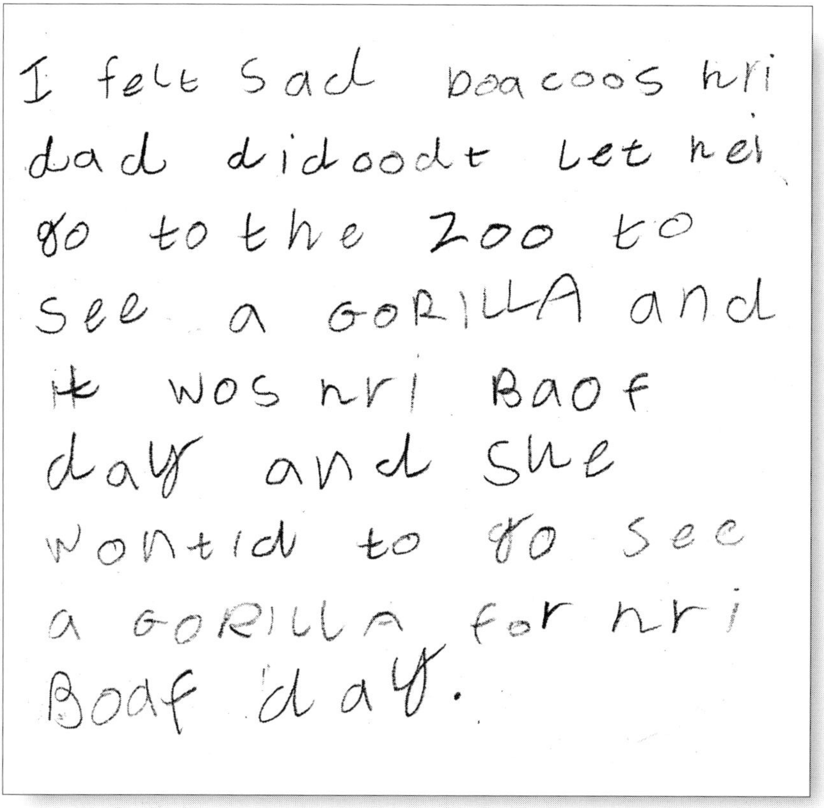

I felt sad beacoos hri dad didoodt Let hei go to the zoo to see a GORILLA and it wos hri Baof day and she wontid to go see a GORILLA for hri Boaf day.

Fig. 2: "I felt sad because her dad didn't let her go to the zoo to see a gorilla and he was horrible all day and she wanted to go [and] see a gorilla for her birthday."

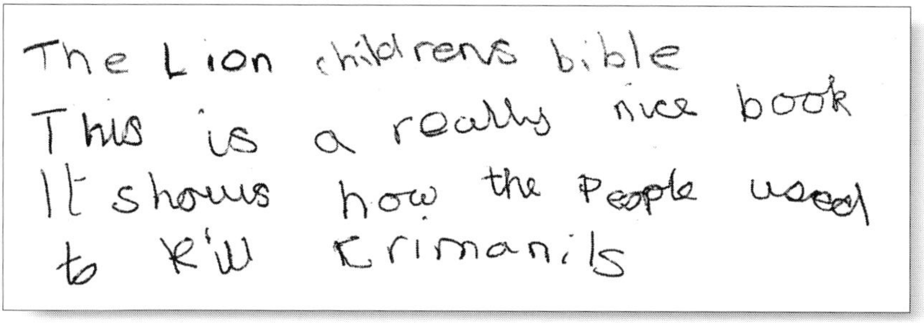

The Lion childrens bible This is a really nice book It shows how the People used to kill crimanils

Fig. 3: "This is a really nice book. It shows how the people used to kill criminals."

Another common type of entry in the reading journal concerns parts of the story that were puzzling, or that the writer did not fully understand.

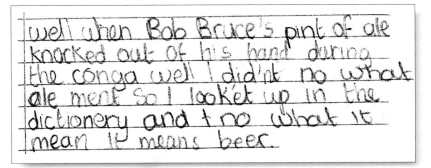

well when Bob Bruce's pint of ale knocked out of his hand during the conga well I did'nt no what ale ment so I looket up in the dictionery and t no what it mean it means beer.

Fig. 4: Sometimes children identify parts of the text that they did not understand.

The teacher should respond regularly to the entries in reading journals, but not to correct what children have said, or how they have said it. Through her comments, the teacher needs to establish the kind of dialogue with each pupil that encourages the full range of responses to reading. Sometimes this will simply be an encouraging comment and at other times a more specific response will be required:

I really enjoyed reading your comments;
I can really see how you are thinking as you read;
I agree I think this is a boring book but I know lots of children like it,
 I wonder why!?
I'm really sorry you don't write in here more often;
Instead of telling the story, think about the pictures you imagine
 when you read;
Re- read to see if your ideas have changed.

To introduce children to the reading journal, use the book you are reading aloud to the class. Show the book and discuss the cover, title and author. Ask the class for questions and predictions about the story. Then, read the first page and ask the class for more questions and predictions. Who will be the main character? How do they know? What kind of book is this? How do they know? What will happen next? How do they know? What questions come into their minds about the story? How do they picture the opening scene?

Write their responses on the board and have them copied into a class journal that can be added-to and re-read as the story progresses. As you read the book, try to ensure that all children have their turn at deciding what gets written into the reading journal, perhaps choosing two or three different children each day. At intervals, re-read the journal aloud to see if questions have been answered or ideas changed. Encourage children to respond in a variety of ways in the journal, using maps of journeys or houses, family trees, time lines, or try asking them to illustrate a particular scene or character, comparing their ideas and discussing the reasons for differences.

Use the reading journal to help the children to see that they are actively involved in the reading. Only give them individual journals when you feel that they are completely ready. It is a good idea to continue to use the class journal until the practice is well established. If you rush into individual journal writing you may be disappointed when nothing happens, and give up.

Chapter 3

Literature Circles with Younger Children

The following examples are drawn from working with a group of six and seven year-old children, who had been selected because they were not achieving as well as their peers. The teacher hoped that additional experiences would enhance their progress as readers.

I met with them for 12 sessions over four months, each session lasting approximately 20-30 minutes. I provided the texts and we always began by discussing the cover of the chosen book. After that, I read the first page or two to help them into the 'tune of the text'. Thereafter the children read round the group aloud, in turn, until we were well into the story, when they were asked to read one or two pages silently to themselves. I provided a question to focus this silent reading.

I did not have specific learning intentions other than to help the children to read and discuss a selection of texts where the illustrations played a key role. Initially I led most of the talk, but as the children became familiar with me and with the idea of a literature circle, they began to talk and respond to each other without my intervention. The following extracts provide a snap shot of this process and of my changing role within the group.

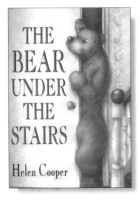

The Bear Under The Stairs:
Introducing the story

The Bear Under The Stairs by Helen Cooper (Puffin) is a tale about William, a young boy who is scared of the dark space under the stairs. He simply knows there is a great big bear living there.

Amy	*I know* (the title *The Bear under the Stairs*)
CK	*Right don't open it for the moment*
Others	*The Bear under the... 'The Bear Under the Stairs'*
CK	*What do we think? ... Oliver, what do you think the book might be about?*
Mark	*There's a bear under the stairs*
CK	*It's about... Well it says"Bear under the Stairs"*
Anne	*He looks evil*
Amy	*He looks grumpy*
CK	*Don't open it please* (to Mark)
Amy	*He looks cross*
CK	*You think he looks evil and grumpy? Let me see you looking like the bear.*
	(They all look cross and grumpy)
CK	*Right, O.K. Do you think.... What makes him look grumpy and evil then?*
Mark	*His fur*
Anne	*He looks evil because of his eyebrows that go like...*
Amy	*Yes, and he's got and if you took his... away*
Anne	*And it's like an evil smile*
Amy	*No but if you took that that bit off... it would look like a little small bear but when he has that bit...*
CK	*I see. That's very clever of you, Amy. Let's put our hands over the bit. Does it make a difference if you take that bit over? Does it make him look nicer?*
Jack	*Yeah* (hesitantly)
CK	*Well lets find out.*

We always start by looking at the cover to help children to predict what the book may be about. This helps them to read since they may have some idea of structure, theme and vocabulary. I try not to direct their thinking by too many prescribed questions. I want to see what they suggest themselves. Using an instant drama technique to get the children to act out the bear's expression helps them to think about how the character is feeling and, perhaps, bring their own experiences to the text. Throughout the exchange, the children listen and respond to each other as they all engage in joint meaning making. Amy and Anne build on Mark's suggestion about what makes the bear look cross and Amy's final suggestion, with its hint that the bear might not be as cross as he looks, makes everyone look again and in more detail. I encourage everyone to contribute and when necessary slow the conversation down to allow everyone time to think. I ask Amy to evidence her suggestion about the bear's face, and use Amy's and Jack's contributions to frame a question that will help everyone to think about the story as they read.

The Bear Under The Stairs: Reading the text

CK   *Anne you said "scared for the place under the stairs". Did you mean to say that? What does it say?*

Amy   *Of*

CK   *Yes those little words... we often get them mixed up. Okay, Amy would you like to read the next page for us please*

Amy   *William*

CK   *William... now that's a bit tricky that word*

Amy   *worried*

CK   *Good girl - worried*

Amy   *William worried about the bear. He worried.* (This is a miscue – the text reads wondered.)

CK   *No... try it...*

Liz   *I know*

Amy   *'wondered that'...*

CK   *Yes. He wondered....*

Amy   *... that it might*

CK   *he wondered...*

Amy   *...what it might be. Yum, Yum the bear...*

CK   *Can you read it as though the bear was saying "Yum Yum"? Go on.*

Amy   *"Yum Yum" the bear said in William's head. "I'm a very hungry bear"* (pauses at the next word (perhaps))

Mark   *I think I know what's on the next page*

CK   *'I'm a very hungry bear per... per...'*

Amy   *Per...*

CK   *What's the second little word in there? You've got the first bit. Read the rest of the sentence, Amy.* (pause)

CK   *I'm a very hungry bear 'something', I'll eat...*

Amy   *boys for tea*

CK	*Per...* (to the rest of the group) *Help her out*
Anne	*perhaps*
CK	*Yes Right okay. Why does it say "the bear in William's head", Amy?* (Pause) *What about you, Liz?*
Liz	*Umm... cos*
CK	*You think you know?*
Liz	*Cos he's thinking the bear's saying it*
Liz	*Can we keep that book to read it again? Can you bring it back please?*

This is a difficult text for these children, and my role in this part of the literature circle was primarily helping them to persist, and to read for meaning whilst paying close attention to the words. During the dialogue, I repeat Anne's reading so that she can hear her miscue, and Amy helps her out. I invite Amy to continue the reading. Initially, Amy reads that instead of what and I repeat what she says to prompt her to self correct, which she does. Amy doesn't read with expression, and I try to encourage her to do so because it will help her to listen to herself as she reads and thus help her comprehension. Hearing others read with expression in the literature circle will also help her. I know that Amy cannot read the word perhaps and try cueing her in by reading the whole sentence, omitting just the problematic word. This time, Anne, who has been listening and had to focus less on decoding the words, helps Amy and suggests a word that makes sense and fits the look of the word on the page.

There is a question about whether the bear is imaginary or real. This doubt is one aspect that makes the book intriguing for the children. Liz is first to suggest that the bear is imaginary. The others are not quite sure. After quiet reading of a key passage, I asked if the bear really did exist, or not. Four children agreed that the bear was real, and went back through the book pointing to the bear in the pictures, saying "The bear is nearly in every single page". Only Liz insists "No, the boy's imagining it".

The intellectual and emotional pull of the book is clear at the end, when Liz asks if they can keep the book to read again. Wanting to re-visit and re-read is the hallmark of a good book. Although not often a request made of reading scheme books, it is vital for both the children's reading skills and their understanding. On re-reading, the children will be more accurate and fluent, and will revisit the big questions, such as whether the bear is real. Providing young children with sufficient opportunities to re-read books in school, because the want to re-read them, is important.

Ghost Train:
A self-reliant community of readers

Ghost Train by Allan Ahlberg (Puffin) is the story of three skeletons on a ghost-train in a dark, dark tunnel in the dead of night. The joke at the end of the book is that a human baby, rather than any of the scary monsters, scares the three skeletons and makes them all run to hide in bed.

Jack	*I keep thinking they used to be robbers (referring to the skeletons)*
CK	*I wonder what makes you think that?... Does anyone want to say anything about these skeletons?*
Mark	(Reading from the book) *They watched the Monster's Beauty Parade* (Mark laughs)
CK	*You think that's funny? Why?*
Mark	*Cos monsters aren't beautiful, are they?*

Later in the same session the children read a line of text written in the book as "very very dark, dark..."

Jack	*Why has it got a line under there?*
CK	*Why has it?*
Amy	*Cos it's very, very*
Anne	*Cos you're supposed to say it like...*
CK	*How would you say it then?*
Anne	*VERY*
Mark	*On the next page I think we're going to find out what it is*
CK	*What frightened the skeletons then? Why is that funny?*
Amy	*Cos they frighten people. They shouldn't be scared*
CK	*What scared them, Mark?*

Mark	*The baby - cos it was so loud*
CK	*So what did they do?*
Mark	*They ran home and got under the bed*
Anne	*Like 'We're going on a Bear Hunt'*
CK	*Yes indeed*

When Jack links robbers and skeletons, he is making his own connections and I invite more explanation. Mark sees the story differently, and his laughter and explanation helps the others to see the joke. I don't answer Jack's question about why the second very has been underlined because I want them to start looking to each other for answers rather than being dependent on the teacher. Standing back in this way also allows me to assess what they know. Mark's next contribution, "On the next page I think we're going to find out what it is" indicates not only excitement about the story, but also a sense that the group is a community, all engaged in the same quest for meaning. When I asked, "What frightened the monsters?", I didn't expect Amy's answer. I was expecting Mark's response as the obvious one. This is a good illustration of the different ways that children interpret stories. Anne's final comment links this book with another text read and will help everyone to recognise this type of story genre.

Janet & Allan Ahlberg

Burglar Bill:
Thinking critically about the story

Burglar Bill by Allan Ahlberg (Puffin) is a story of Bill, a burglar by trade. Everything in his life is stolen. One night he steals a box with holes in the lid, only to discover he has stolen a baby. Later, Bill is himself burgled, by Burglar Betty. She is the mother of the baby. Bill and Betty decide to reform, live honest lives and get married. The discussion overleaf occurred when the children were looking at a picture of Burglar Bill stealing women's clothes.

Jack	*What's the point of having girl's things?*
CK	*That's a good point. Why steal things for girls?*
Anne	*Disguise himself as a girl?*
CK	*Oh well there we go, possibly. Maybe he does...*
Jack	*Why would he disguise himself in girls' things?*
Anne	*Cos he's a robber and he has to disguise himself*
CK	*Lets see what happens... Come on Liz, read the next page for us*

Jack notices something in picture that I had never thought about. When he questions the text in this way, we all learn to look at it anew. Anne hypothesises and answers Jack's question without looking to the teacher to intervene. Such exchanges, which occur throughout, show how the children have established themselves as a true literature circle, and are really listening to, and learning from, each other.

The Children's Views

When I asked this group of inexperienced readers what they thought about being members of a Literature Circle there was, unsurprisingly, a strong focus on words:

Mark	*You get to learn to read big words because I think I've never read books like that before*
Jack	*Because they've got hard words. The books we have, have easy words*
CK	*What about when you're' looking at the pictures and you've all got different ideas, is that good?*
Anne	*Because you're very imaginative*
Liz	*And you're thinking*
CK	*Is it different from when you have group reading in the class?*
Jack & Anne	*Yes. Because you bring in lots of books*
Anne	*And they are really nice because you can look at the pages. You can spend a long time looking at them and it's, like, in the classroom you don't really have a lot of time and there's not a lot of things to look at...*
Liz	*We only normally read half of the book. In this group we read the whole*

Anne   ...*You don't really look at the pictures because there's not really anything to look at*

Liz   *The books you bring are really quite interesting*

Mark   ... *and funny*

These responses demonstrate the children's appreciation of quality texts and their desire to read more complex stories and 'hard words' as well as the confidence that came from children reading successfully within a group. The responses also show the children's need to set their own pace for studying the book – allowing sufficient time to talk and time to look at the pictures. All five children easily met the national expectations for seven year-olds. Importantly, the child who began as an able reader of words but with little interest in reading, became an involved meaning maker – especially of funny books.

Chapter 3

Literature Circles with 8-11 Year Olds

The role of talk in reading

Within my class of 10 year-old children, there is a strong emphasis on talk, about literature. Because the reading process involves the cre- ntal images in the mind, children's understanding of what they enhanced through discussion with others. When children read, or hear stories read to them, they discover that the story stays within their ımething like a memory" (Meek, 1991), and talking about those ages and the feelings evoked by the text can lead to greater ding. When such talk happens, the children and the teacher are negotiating meaning together.

I am also very aware of the need to model the reading process for the children. Hence, when we read, I talk about how I am drawing on my knowledge of spoken and written language, of life and of other books I have read. In doing this, I try to show them what happens inside the reader's head.

Fire, Bed & Bone:
Exploring the text together

Fire, Bed & Bone by Henrietta Branford (Walker Books) is a dramatic tale of the Peasants' Revolt, set in England in 1381. The story is narrated by an old hunting dog who is given all a dog could want - fire, bed and bone - by her peasant owners, Rufus and Comfort, and their children. The story tells how the rebellion against the hardship and injustice of oppressive landlords spreads among the peasants of southern England, and how their lives change dramatically.

We began our first session by reading the opening chapter of *Fire, Bed and Bone* and I asked who might be telling the story. One child suggested that it might be a wolf. Another replied passionately: " It can't possibly be a wolf!" When asked to explain why not, his response included reference to the whole picture in his mind of the domestic scene: adults and their children curled up asleep and the baby reaching out to touch the narrator (with no reference to her fearing it). He continued to talk about the language of the story, saying: "A wolf wouldn't say '*the wolves* came down to the farm', and it does it later too… '*their* voices', it's as if it's talking about *someone*, *things*, that are different to it.". Other children contributed, using evidence from the text to support their interpretations, which they were clearly relating to their own experiences. The group reached the conclusion, between them, that the narrator was probably a dog, being an animal that was part of the family, but also because dogs would explore the outside worlds described. As they talked, the children were very clearly describing the 'other worlds', as they had constructed them within their heads, and using these to make sense of the text.

My role in the literature circle discussion varied. Throughout, I listened, questioned, and responded with my own thoughts, and at times I indicated to individuals that they needed to listen to each other, modelling how engrossed I was in what the children had to say. At other times I questioned, asking what a particular child or pair of children thought, and why. Sometimes I intervened to help the group move on, by asking what pictures they each had in their heads. Sometimes I re-read key sections of the text out loud, stressing certain elements to draw attention to them. Other times I described how I felt, and what impact the writing had on my thoughts. I was also aware of how I was communicating my enjoyment of the discussion and how impressed I was with the children's engagement and their thoughtfulness. At other times I simply gave them time and space to think their own thoughts, then share them with a response partner within the group.

This first session was typical of the sessions that followed. The children translated the pictures in their minds into words, in order to share them. They could be seen thinking: frowning, concentrating, catching their breath, starting to speak, then stopping and continuing to think before finally speaking again.

I had assumed that this was the process of inner speech being expressed for others; external speech stopping abruptly as they returned to their own inner thoughts (Vygotsky, 1962). On reflection, I question how much of their external speech was being shaped by their need to communicate ideas to the others. At times the children appeared to be thinking out loud, and the language was changed to accommodate their shifting thoughts. It wasn't always being changed to help others understand. Sometimes, when I was silent and really listening to individuals, this process was more apparent: a child appeared to be making sense of her/his thoughts orally, not explaining them to me but voicing them at me, because I was listening. There was much evidence of language and thinking being inextricably linked in the struggle to communicate ones' understanding to others (Wells, 1986).

I was very aware of how I listened to the children and then structured my questions to take them further. I was also aware that by drawing the children's attention to key elements of the text, I was asking them to consider issues that had not previously been discussed and were possibly new to them.

Eventually, I drew the children back to the opening two sentences: '*The wolves came down to the farm last night. They spoke to me of freedom*'. We considered why the writer had opened the story in this way. Again, I assume that my questioning forced the children to think, to draw on their knowledge of life, other texts and personal experience (Britton, 1970). The children presented various hypotheses about the nature of the story, mostly to do with animals in captivity and the possibility of the wolves freeing the dog from domesticity. Again, they drew on the text to support their theories, again I saw them using language to communicate thinking and their thinking being challenged by each other's words. They grappled with vague knowledge about life 'a long time ago', with images from the story of people who lived in poverty working on farms, and of powerful rich people living in relative luxury being prompted by the reference to the 'Great House'. Each child contributed his or her own ideas about the setting and period, contributing the snippets of information brought from inside their heads. It was like watching a jigsaw puzzle being put together, each piece adding to the overall picture that they were creating. As they talked about their understanding of the period and of the novel, I saw their thinking challenged by the language of the text.

The literature circles discussion also provided an excellent basis for collaborative writing, and the children produced some fantastic poetry:

I know many different worlds:
The house, village and the wildwoods.
I know the places of comfort and the places
To hide.

I am a hunting dog.

The wolves call, far out by the pine trees.
I do not fear them.

Tomorrow is the day

Humble creeps in, soft as smoke.
My back aches.
The fire wraps its warmth around me
And I sleep.

By Emmet & Mathew

Fig. 5: Collaborative poem by Emmet and Mathew

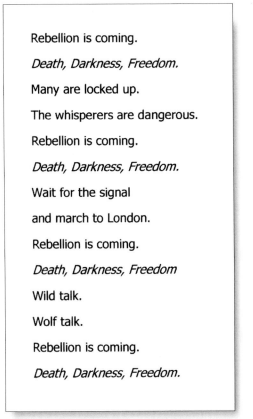

Rebellion is coming.

Death, Darkness, Freedom.

Many are locked up.

The whisperers are dangerous.

Rebellion is coming.

Death, Darkness, Freedom.

Wait for the signal

and march to London.

Rebellion is coming.

Death, Darkness, Freedom

Wild talk.

Wolf talk.

Rebellion is coming.

Death, Darkness, Freedom.

Fig. 6: Collaborative poem by Shawnu, Tabitha and Emma

Using the Reading Journals

The children recorded their thoughts in reading journals, as they read. This was not an entirely silent task: they often interrupted the silence in their eagerness to voice the thoughts, which appeared to have been generated by writing in their reading journal, as well as by reading the text. I had modelled the process of keeping a reading journal by describing to the children how sometimes my thoughts seemed to drop off the end of my pen without me really realising that I had had them. The children used their reading journals to think about their reactions to the story.

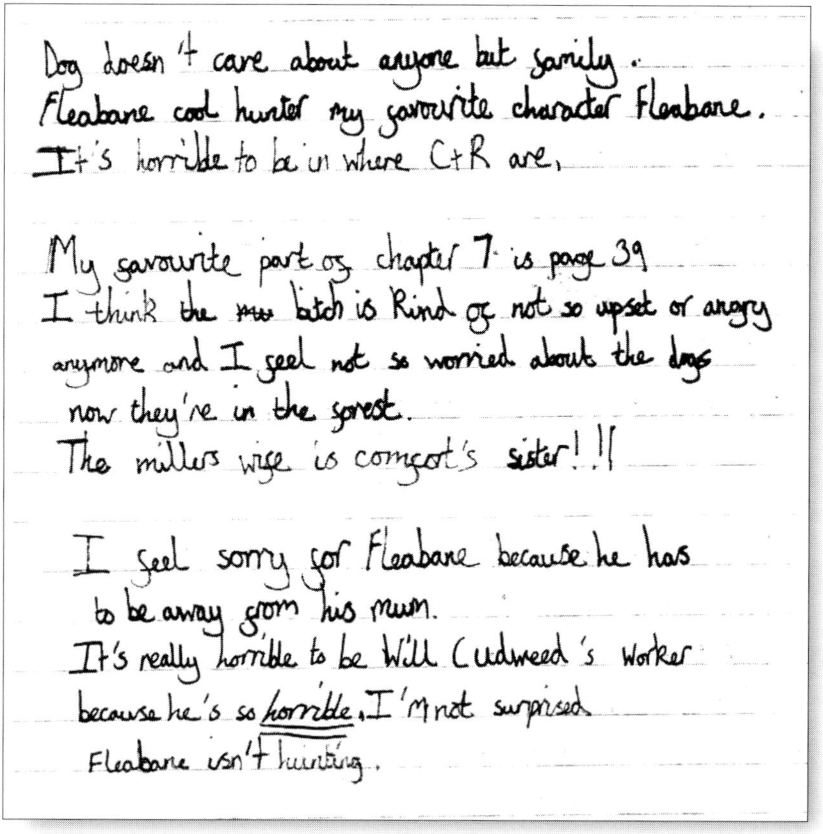

Dog doesn't care about anyone but family.
Fleabane cool hunter my favourite character Fleabane.
It's horrible to be in where C+R are.

My favourite part of chapter 7 is page 39
I think the mu bitch is kind of not so upset or angry
anymore and I feel not so worried about the dogs
now they're in the forest.
The millers wife is comfort's sister! !!

I feel sorry for Fleabane because he has
to be away from his mum.
It's really horrible to be Will Cudweed's worker
because he's so _horrible_, I'm not surprised
Fleabane isn't hunting.

Fig. 7: Children use reading journals to think about their reactions to the story

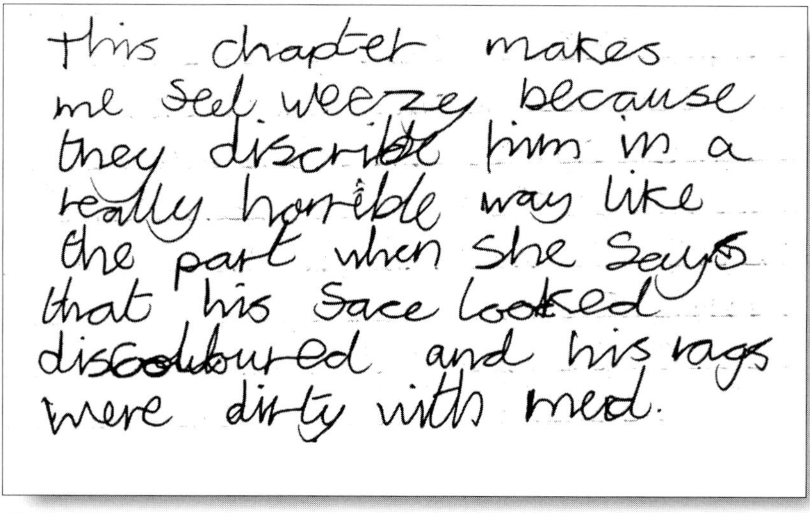

this chapter makes
me feel weeze because
they discribe him in a
really horrible way like
the part when she says
that his face looked
discolbured and his rags
were dirty with med.

Fig. 8: Children use reading journals to think about their reactions to the story

Robinson and King (1995) stress how this type of writing can help children develop their thinking. One child wrote:

> Rebellion is coming.
> The whisperers = Some maybe good some maybe spies
> Rufus told wrong people.
> Whisperers want greedom but some want trouble.

Fig. 9: "Rebellion is coming. The whisperers = some may be good some may be spies. Rufus told wrong people. Whisperers want freedom but some want trouble."

Another started writing then suddenly gasped and said, "I've just realised something", to which I replied, "write it down, don't lose the thought. You can share it with the rest when we've all finished writing". He had written:

> 20/3/02
> at the begining wolves talk of freedom. now it sais "...end to serfdom
> wild talk. wolfs talk.

Fig. 10: "At the beginning, [of the book] wolves talk of freedom. Now it says 'end to serfdom'. Wild talk = wolf talk.

In both these examples the children were writing to make sense of what they had read, but through their writing, they were also shaping their thoughts and making new meanings (D'Arcy, 1989). Their writing then helped them reflect upon their thoughts, to share them with the others. I found that the discussion after writing in their reading journals was much more collaborative than earlier sessions, with each child contributing to the flow of ideas as they grappled to make sense of what was happening in the story. We were able to reach agreed decisions about the peasants and the coming rebellion, and we were able to use the second child's thoughts to help us consider the references to wolves and the opening lines of the book. We really were "talking ourselves into understanding" (Winchester, 1985, p.68).

My role was crucial. As the children wrote their thoughts, so I wrote mine. When we discussed the chapters, I shared my thoughts along with the children. I didn't feel as if we were a group of children with a teacher, I felt that we were all learners and teachers together. I learned from them and they learned from me. We shared our experience of reading the text. We shared our experience of writing our thoughts. We talked about how the text made us feel and what we thought was yet to come. We responded to each other's thoughts and ideas. Wells (1986) stresses the importance of the teacher really listening to children because of a belief that what they have to say is important. He highlights the way in which questions are used, not to check that the children's understanding conforms to the teacher's, but for the teacher to be further informed.

Our Final Thoughts

Later work in the literature circle included drama and writing in role. The children were highly motivated to write: their exploration of the text through talk and drama gave them a voice and something to say. Their consideration of the way in which Henrietta Branford's writing had impacted on them as readers significantly enhanced the quality of their writing. The overriding message for me was the power of talking about literature, together, in ways that bring the text to life.

I asked the children about what they thought about the value of literature circles. Some valued the opportunity to set their own agenda and discuss their own reactions and thoughts:

They give me a chance to talk about what I think about the book

Others valued the collaborative nature of the discussion because it helped them to develop new understandings:

There are more brains for more ideas

(You can) discover different ideas, lets you understand more, fit different pieces together, you remember what's happened

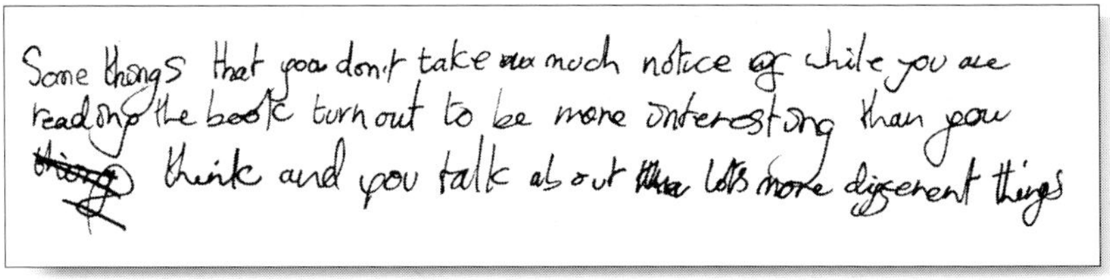

Some things that you don't take much notice of while you are reading the book turn out to be more intersting than you ~~thing~~ think and you talk about lots more digerent things

Fig. 11: "Some things that you don't take much notice of while you are reading the book turn out to be more interesting than you think, and you talk about lots of different things."

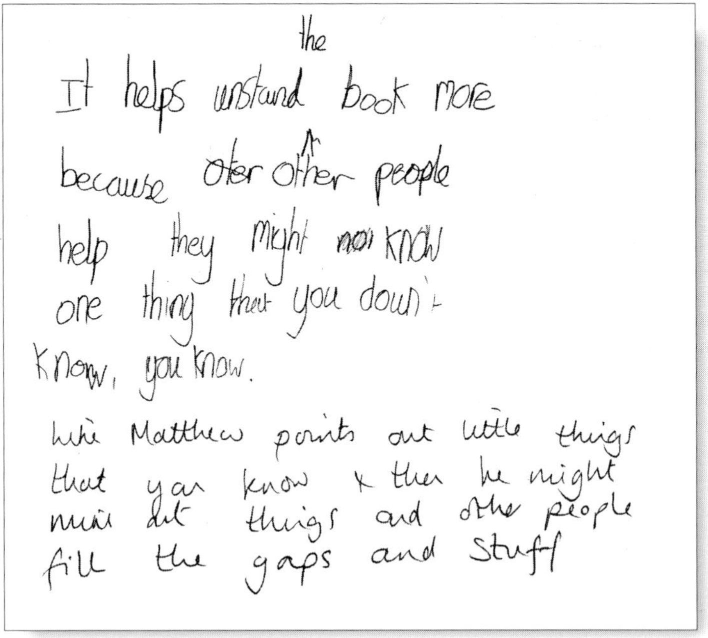

It helps unstand the book more because ~~oter~~ other people help they might not know one thing that you dount know, you know.

like Matthew points out little things that you know & then he might miss out things and other people fill the gaps and stuff

Fig. 12: "It helps [you] understand the book more because other people help - they might know one thing that you don't know you know… like Matthew points out little things that you know and then he might miss out things and other people fill the gaps"

I am, now, even more than ever, in agreement with Robinson and King (1995) about the power of literature circles to develop children a readers, writers and thinkers… and with Matthew (aged 10) wh wrote a list, ending with the most powerful thought of all:

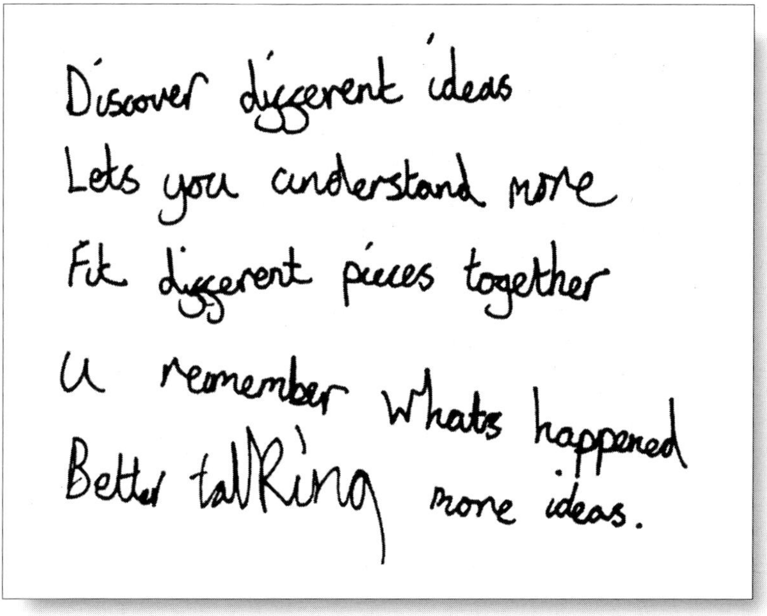

Discover different ideas
Lets you understand more
Fit different pieces together
U remember whats happened
Better talking more ideas.

Fig. 13: "Better talking more ideas".

Bibliography

Barnes, D. (1976) *From Communication to Curriculum.* Harmondsworth: Penguin

Britton, J. (1970) *Language and Learning.* London: Penguin

Britton, J., Burgess, A., Martin, N., Macleod, A. & Rosen, H. (1975) *The Development of Writing Abilities, 11-18.* London: Macmillan

Britton, J. (1982) 'Writing to Learn and Learning to Write' in Pradl, G. (ed.) *Prospect and Retrospect: Selected Essays of James Britton.* London: Heinemann Educational

DfEE Standards and Effectiveness Unit (1998) *Literacy Training Pack* (video 1) London: DfEE

DfEE Standards and Effectiveness Unit (1998) *The National Literacy Strategy: Frame work for Teaching.* London: DfEE

DfEE (1999) *English: The National Curriculum for England, Key Stages 1- 4.* London: QCA

D'Arcy, P. (1989) *Making Sense, Shaping Meaning.* London: Heinemann Primary

Graham, L (1999) *'Changing Practice through reflection: The KS2 Reading project, Croydon'* in Reading. 33 (3) p.106-113

King, C. & Robinson, M. (1993) *Creating a Community of Readers Parts 1 & 2: Videos and Teachers Notes.* Brighton: Brighton University Media Services

Harste, J. Short, K. and Burke, C. (1989) *Creating Classrooms for Authors: The Reading-Writing Connection.* Portsmouth, NH: Heinemann Educational

Meek, M. (1982) *Learning to Read.* London: Bodley Head

Meek, M. (1991) *On Being Literate.* London: Bodley Head

Paul, A. (1995) *Can Key Stage One Children Operate Independently in Literature Circles?* Unpublished B.A. Dissertation. University of Brighton

Robinson, M. & King C. (1995) 'Creating a Community of Readers' *English in Education* 29 (2)

Rosenblatt, L. M. (1978) *The Reader, the Text and the Poem: The Transactional Theory of Poetry.* Carbondale, IL: Southern Illinois University Press.

Vygotsky, L. (1962) *Thought and Language.* Cambridge, MA: MIT Press

Vygotsky, L. (1978) *Mind in Society.* Cambridge, MA: Harvard University Press.

Walton, S. (1998) *Literature Circles: A Strategy For Motivating The Reluctant Reader.* Unpublished B.A. Dissertation. University of Brighton.

Wells, G. 1986: *The Meaning Makers.* Portsmouth, NH: Heinemann

Winchester, S. 1985: Learning Through Talk: Classroom Applications in B.Wade (Ed) *Talking to Some Purpose.* Edgebaston: University of Birmingham

Resource note

Two videos *Creating Communities of Readers part 1 and 2* are designed to support teachers who want to introduce literature circles into their class practice. Part One focuses on four to five year-old children and covers a range of reading approaches, including literature circles. Part Two focuses on nine and ten year old children and tracks the progress one group of readers made across the school year, as members of a literature circle. Available from Pam Blackman Curriculum Centre Bevendean House University of Brighton FalmerBN1 9PH.
Email: Pam Blackman @bton.ac.uk

Children's books

Blume, J. 1982: *It's not the end of the World.* London: Heinemann Educational

Browne. A. 1983: *Gorilla.* London: Walker Books

Impey, R. 1992: *Trouble with The Tucker Twins.* London: Viking

Mahy, M. 1990: *The Haunting.* London: Mammoth

Swindells, R. 1992: *The Ice Palace.* London: Young Puffin Story Books

Final Advice

Read the book once and if you don't understand it properly use what you know to understand it. When summer will comes there are more brains for more ideas.

UKLA MINIBOOKS

Drama: Reading, Writing and Speaking Our Way Forward

By Teresa Grainger and Angela Pickard

Do you want to motivate and involve your class? Do you want to make more use of drama in your literacy teaching? This accessible and inspiring book can help. It provides ideas, support and insights to enable you to plan drama, both within your English time and across the curriculum. It highlights what children learn through drama and how drama can contribute to their development as readers, writers, speakers and listeners. With practical strategies and classroom examples, this book offers imaginative ways forward for teachers and children alike.

About the Authors

Teresa Grainger is a Reader in Education at Canterbury Christ Church University College where she leads an MA programme in literacy and learning. Her research currently involves investigating the relationship between drama and writing, children's voice and verve in writing and the nature of creative teaching. Her most recent book is *Creativity and Writing; Developing Voice and Verve in the Classroom* with Goouch, K. and Lambirth, A. (2005, Routledge).

Angela Pickard is a Senior lecturer in Education at Canterbury Christ Church University College. She teaches on undergraduate, postgraduate and continuing professional development programmes. Her research interests include role play areas and drama, small group interaction, dance and physical literacies.

Drama: Reading, Writing and
Speaking Our Way Forward

By Teresa Grainger
and Angela Pickard

Minibook 18

Minibooks are available from

UKLA Publications,

Upton House, 4 Baldock Street

Royston, Hertfordshire SG8 5AY

UKLA MINIBOOKS

Tell Me Another...
Speaking, Listening and Learning Through Storytelling

By Jacqueline Harrett

Storytelling techniques not only enhance the speaking and listening skills of children, they help change children from superficial, deceptive or even inattentive listeners into more participatory and reflective listeners and learners who may also become more creative thinkers.

This book explains how teachers may use storytelling throughout the curriculum to enable children to become effective, powerful learners.

About the Author

Jacqueline Harrett is currently a senior lecturer at the Cardiff School of Education and has extensive classroom experience at both primary and secondary levels. She is undertaking research for a PhD on the responses of children to storytelling and story-reading. The ideas in this book stem from her classroom practice and observations, both as a teacher and researcher.

Minibooks are available from

UKLA Publications,

Upton House, 4 Baldock Street

Royston, Hertfordshire SG8 5AY

For more details of the United Kingdom Literacy Association see the association website at **www.ukla.org**